A

GIRL

LIKE

NO

OTHER

A GIRL LIKE NO OTHER

Author's name
Esther Muir

Editors: thank you
To my lovely Editor.

Cover illustrations - Esther

Description:

A real-life account of journey from the villages of
rural Kenya to living in the lively hustle and bustle of
Nairobi, then adjusting to London, a global city with
new adjustments and cultures.
Bahati's life has seen grief, struggle and success, but
through all has maintained a strength and optimism
through life which has seen her far.

Started on 10/08/2020

Editorial Reviews:

Authors Bio
A dynamic author who uses life experience in two different countries to highlight the home and working life, and the struggle and joys associated readers will enjoy the relatable stories and also a look back into time growing up in a rural Kenya.

SYPNOSIS

As a young girl

This book is written in a third-party version by the creator of this book being the character thus no copy write permission is needed by the writer from anybody. The writer is the actual character to make it the way the writer wanted.

This girl was, Bahati, she was born in a very loving home and was waited for as the parents had 5 boys before she was born. Three of those brothers died of childhood illness, she was born in a farm with farm animals which she loved very much.

Lockdown 2020 has provided enough time to reflect and write this book after all bittersweet memories came flooding in Bahati's head.

BAHATI'S LIFE

Bahati's home was unfit for habitation considering all aspect of safety as it did not have water or lights, the walls were not insulated and had no heating. Her parents had nine children and had lost three of the children due to childhood illnesses. Those babies that died were from their marriage. The family were peasants and were surviving in a tough way.

Those babies that died were at their start of their marriage.
Bahati's family were poor but humble and God fearing. Her whole family was Christian and that was their hope for everything. Faith and belief of God was unshakeable and very important to their life's day to day.

The home was poor but come to think of it now, it wasn't that bad as her father owned the land and home that she grew in. There was a lot of life, laugh happiness and storytelling with the family its indescribable.

She was loved a great deal to the point of being spoilt due to the fact that the parents had 5 boys before she was born. During those days, there was no good healthcare. When she was around 7 or 8, she remembers seeing her mum being sick all the time, but she did not understand what the problem was. Later, she learnt that her mum had blood pressure and diabetes. To return to this chapter.

Bahati attended the village primary school that was a long distance. She had to cross the river through the stone bridge, no bridge was available at the time. She was always scared to cross the river as river would fill up during rainy season and it would dry up during dry seasons. The primary school was so far the children could not understand why a primary school would be so far. Of cause, after bahati grew older she realized that the government wasn't improving the local community by building schools. Every day on her way from school, she would be suffering from headaches due to dehydration and long walks.

Bahati and her friends remembers vividly how they would divert in bushes looking for wild raspberries and blackberries. This was a regular activity on their way from school during those early years which they enjoyed very much. Even though the primary school was so far, she had the best time playing on the way back from school as that was the easy part of her life and most her other friends.

Bahati never had shoes during her primary school days.
The first pair of shoes was bought for her when she was going to secondary school from Bata shoes shop, was when she was going to her boarding secondary school. Her and other friends played outside without shoes, too and it was normal to play bare foot during that time.

She remembers how she was handed old clothes by people from the church when she was young. The clothes were worn out and wrong sizes, mostly oversize but she never complained or refused the clothes. Even though now people still hand down old clothes, it was seen as poverty to be given old clothes by friends and families at that time.

Bahati was God fearing girl and she never missed a Sunday service; she was in choir group and enjoyed bible stories immensely. She was a very happy and joyous young girl she was liked by everyone including the teachers, friends and mostly her parents.

Bahati had one worry that kept her anxious all the time. Her mum had diabetes and blood pressure, but she did not know that the illness was serious to kill her mum one day due to luck of treatment.

Since her mum was always unwell most times and could not attend the Sunday service, Bahati would listen to the whole service so that when she went back home, she would repeat it all over again for her mother. Listening to the service and then going through it all over again for her mum and this made Bahati understand the Bible more. She

belonged to the church choir and enjoyed attending practice early before the church. It was

most enjoyable because she and the choir members all attended the same school, so they had a tight friendship.

She was also very petrified of finding snakes on the way to school which is her biggest phobia, so she walked with her brothers and other children all the time.

Bahati was a very happy and joyous young girl. She enjoyed playing netball and running around and also hide and seek with her friends.

But Bahati had one worry that kept her worried all the time. Her mum had diabetes and blood pressure but at that young age she did not know what was wrong with her mum.

That time there wasn't good healthcare for blood pressure and diabetes. You can imagine that's the

most preventable lifestyle decease but there wasn't enough research invested into that area. Her mum loved her very much and used to make her hand-made school uniform which was a tunic dress blouse and a knitted cardigan. Her mum used to make her a very long skirt which she did not like especially when she was year ten and over.
Bahati knew how to stitch clothes by hand using needle and thread just like designers do.
She would hide in her bedroom and shorten her school skirt by hand using needle and thread just as she used to see her mother stitching. (She has treasured those small memories).

After school Bahati would go straight in the bedroom and change so that her mum does not notice that she altered the length of the school skirt. This practice gave bahati a liking to making clothes when she grew older. She bought a Singer sewing machine, but these dreams did not go far. Her sewing interest faded away as more interesting things attracted her.

Bahati was starting to be very responsible since her mum was unwell, she would do all the house chores, those days children would not dare to refuse to do their chores plus the kitchen work. So, she knew how to prepare the few menu items that were available.

Bahati was very bright in school too even though she worried about her mother's illness all the time. She had many friends and used to go and play in the fields with her friends. Her father had a big farm with so many farm animals, cows, goats and chickens, cat and a dog.

She had no toys to play with or anything like that, they just played running around, games, hide and seek, climbing trees and playfights.

The best thing was that she and her friends did not realise that there were things known as toys or sweets. So, life was indeed very good for them.

Another thing Bahati and her friends did not know sweets. So, she and her friends have very good teeth up to now without any fillings or extractions since she had no sweets at her early age, and she maintained that habit once in urban cities.

She remembers clearly how she enjoyed the farm animals of all sorts. The dog was especially fierce to strangers and visitors would have to shout from afar before approaching her home. Bahati used to run and hold the dog when her friends were visiting.

Even though they had a big farm, Bahati's family were poor, they lived on the farm produce only in terms of food. Totally eating organic fruits, vegetables and meat from the farm. The food was healthy and because they did not have money to buy sugary or unhealthy stuff, her sisters and brothers did not realise that the farm food was the healthiest lifestyle.

Bahati's dad's farm was large like 10 or more hectors and very green with foods and cattle. Her dad did not have a proper job so there was no money for the family. All kids were young when their mum died. Behati's dad looked after them all until they grew up. She remembers her dad had another piece of land three miles away known as munanda. The children used to be asked to go and help cultivate on Saturdays. Her big brother

was so mean he would ask Bahati to carry all the gardening tools while he swaggered along the road with pride like he wasn't going to do the gardening. Bahati being the only girl hated it so much, but she was always outnumbered. When they got to the farm, the big brother would be walking around commanding other kids and, in the end, he will escape doing any work. He has never liked dirty work, always a white colour job. He is a hot peri peri type of guy who likes being very smart all the time and he does not have down time.

First forward the kid grew and have since looked after the old man in every way possible, even though there were always the small squabbles here and there as usual with other families. Bahati was blessed financially, hence she contributed f
inancial support, other emotional support and other daily requirements and obviously a very good warm house that Behati built for her dad.

DISASTER STRUCK FOR BAHATI AND FAMILY

When Bahati was in first year of her secondary school, her mother died. This was the worst time for her. She did not know what to do because she was approaching the time that she needed her mother the most at puberty. She now had only her father and the other siblings older and younger. That meant she had no one to guide her and the only option was to carry on blindly with life.

(Bahati's mum had 6 live children and the 3 first died of childhood illnesses and poverty conditions).
Bahati was in a boarding school, and it was very frustrating for her to keep the appearance of being tough and concentrate as it was, because she really just had to move on while her mother was unwell to get on with education, move on with life and literally keeping up the pace.

This was because some kids had come from different towns while others like Bahati came from very rural areas. She was pleasant and made friends easily.

If she was left behind a few steps in any way there was no catching up with the schoolwork. Just in the 1st year of secondary school, second term a report came in at her school that her mother had died. A man from the church was sent to school to go and collect her from school. That man was an elder from a presbyterian church her parents used to attend. Looking back

the man came with no sympathy or empathy and just told her that her mum had died, and he's been sent to pick her. That shattered her like a bullet. Everything was a blur. She remembers rolling herself on the grass crying outside the office after being informed and told to go to the dormitory to pick her stuff.

The lack of sympathy was immense, no one picked or hugged her from the ground, she the teacher or the church elder. Bahati finally picked herself up, went to the dormitory to pick her stuff and went with the elder who came to pick her.

After the funeral, she was stuck in a situation on how to think or tackle difficult situations of loneliness, someone to give her protection, comfort and warmth than can only be found from a mother.

MOTHERLESS LIFE OF A YOUNG GIRL

After reaching home, everything looked different for Bahati, now she was officially motherless early teenage girl. There were so many people in her house. That made it difficult for her to really

realise that she did not have a mother anymore. She had not reached her first period which seems to have been a little late at thirteen. She was very thin and that could have contributed to the hormone development hence late puberty. Bahati was with her mother not long ago before the term began. She talked to her mum girly talk and even she packed some sanitary towels for Bahati.

She asked her mother what that was (since her periods had not started) and her mum told her that she will soon start her periods and how she will use them. It's like she had an instinct. Bahati loved her mum and she afterwards headed back

to boarding school not realising that was the last time to see her mother. Being in a boarding school was horrible for her knowing that she left her mum sick. She was so sad being in a hall where she was residing. She had never been away from home before. Just as

she started getting to know the other kids in the

3rd week, she received the news that her mother was dead, she was heartbroken.
Bahati was in lessons when the office staff came and called her to the office.
When She got there, she saw a familiar face from the church. She knew then that something bad has happened. He was a church elder and not necessary a friend.

The man's name who came to pick Bahati from schools was named as Dickson and he quick

honestly told her what had happens without sugar coating it or sympathy. She remembers She fell down on the ground and rolled down crying. Afterwards he said abruptly, we have to go so that we can catch the public transport to get home.

When they got home there were so many people, friends and family just sitting and hanging there cooking and praying. Bahati was very sad she could not believe that her life was at that point where she had no mother. A day before the funeral, a cousin of Bahati said that he would like to take Bahati and her sister to the Nakuru, about 27 miles so that he can buy them new clothes for funeral. He was driving a car that was a banger even by those days' standard.

They stayed over in town and decided to drive down the following day for the funeral. Bahati was happy with her new dresses and now she was headed for the funeral.
The rural roads by then had potholes and before long the banger car was stuck in the mud and the engine refused to start.

Bahati being a very young girl did not realise that a bad situation was starting to happen.
She thought her big cousins were going to fix the car push it out of the potholes and drive to the funeral. By 2 pm they were still stuck at the same spot and missed the funeral. By the time Bahati's cousins managed to get help it was too late.

When they all got at the funeral, the ceremony was over and family pictures had been taken and all people dispersed. Bahati and her sister did not realise the impact of missing her mother's funeral until later in life when it affected her very badly. She would always think (my lovely mum was dead and buried and she did not attend her funeral).

Bahati went over to her dad and hugged him, and they both started crying. Her dad consoled her and assured her that everything will be ok. Her dad brought some food for her, and she and her sister ate.

They were both very hungry after their cousins delayed them and made them miss the funeral. She had not experienced death in the family and being in rural areas, and her mum being very young with many kids, they always stayed at home in their farm.

Bahati went back to boarding school after one week at home. Her friends welcomed her back in school and they made her feel very comfortable. She can still remember one girl who told everyone that no one should disturb Bahati in any way or shape.

That girl was in 3rd year of secondary school and was feared by the other students because she was a very outspoken and strong girl. The time in school was brilliant as far as she can remember. The years went by quickly and before she knew she had completed her GCSE Level education.

Her dad was a very noble man, very caring and respected man who feared God and worked hard, despite living in peasant lifestyle.

When his wife died, she was ten years younger than him, he was heartbroken. The children were all young and needed a lot of care and soon he found himself being the mather and father of the children. He did not remarry.

This meant that he used to work on his farm, get the food from the farm and cook before children get back from school.
He also learns how to manage the bigger kids, by allocating chores to the kids after school.

Bahati being the only bigger girl amongst the boys, she was allocated helping her dad to prepare fire and food. The bigger kids were allocated to do their chores in the farm.
Sometimes her dad would send her to take the milk to the dairy and at the end of
the month her dad would get paid. She hated that particular chore because it is done very early in the morning.

She remembers one time when she was carrying the milk to the dairy and she fell, all the milk poured. She was petrified but her dad reassured her and said it was just an accident and she

should not worry at all. She did not get in trouble for pouring
the milk for sale.

Bahati was starting to think whether that was it for the rest of her life, carrying out chores, being controlled by the big brothers and wait for a boy/husband to appear and safe her from that life. Furthermore, everyone else was living the same rural lifestyle.

Bahati got lucky when her father's friend told her dad that he will get her a job in the city of Nairobi, about 200 km away from her home.
Her dad had a big land that they used to farm and produce their food and some extra food to sell for upkeep. Bahati's dad used to think he was poor because he wasn't working but owning the farm he had (still owning it) makes him a millionaire in today's money.

He never saw it that way as farming was not seen that way at all in those days. Bahati remembers how she used to feel poor because they lived in the farm and not in urban area.

There was a general shop a good distance which Bahati used to be sent to go and get stuff that

they couldn't get from the farm. Things like salt sugar, oil and soaps etc.
Through the years Bahati was not sent to buy unnecessary things like sugar because it wasn't a necessity. Also, she could not buy sweets and chocolates either.

That meant they took their tea without sugar most times because there was no sugar. So as the shopkeeper woman used to be sarcastic to Bahati whenever she came in the shop. She would ask Bahati sarcastically things like "are you not buying sugar and some sweets today?".

CREDIT IN THE SHOP FOR HER FATHER

Normally Bahati's dad had a page for credit note at the shop and he would settle it at the end of the month when he got paid his little pay. So, the shopkeeper used to say when Bahati entered the shop "hello Bahati did your dad gave you some money for today? Or I write it down in the book as usual?" It was very embarrassing for her because

other people in the shop would hear and know her business. The shop woman was really not nice to Bahati and family because of asking for credit which was to be paid after 4 weeks. She noticed that the shop lady used to be stressed looking at every item Bahati was buying.

Bahati never had sweets when she was young due to that extreme poverty. There was never extra money for sweets or treats and anyway she

did not know sweets taste. She was very happy and content though. This made Bahati's life hard, and she made her promise herself that she was to work hard until she makes it.

Bahati's dad was working for an Englishman by the name of we used to call him Msungu, looking after very many cows and tend them like milking and taking the milk to the dairy.

It was tiring and he got rained on all the time whenever it was raining. Bahati's dad was a very hard working but those days they were paid something like100 shillings per month. That amount was supposed to be large that time.

Bahati got a job in the city of Nairobi.

Bahati was getting used to rural life when her father's friend who worked in Nairobi offered to get a job for her. The job was easily got, and she was taken straight from village to the university and asked to start work immediately.

This was the first bridge that opened for her, and she will never forget it or take it for granted.

She has tried to gift this now old man with gifts, but she never feels like she has done enough compared to how grateful she is even after so many years. She had never been in the city of Nairobi before, so this was very amazing for her. Everything looked bright considering she came from the village where there was no lights and hassle and bustle of the city life.

Bahati went to stay with her cousin, in Nairobi an older cousin who could have passed for her mum. The cousin was good for her, and she stayed there for only 3 months. By this time Bahati was realising that she needs her own freedom and privacy. She had formed friendship with some other girls at her new workplace and she wanted to do as she wanted. Furthermore, this was Bahati's first time to leave home properly.

BAHATIS'S FRIENDS

Her friends loved her so much, they have never before seen a fresh girl from the village. All the friends they used to meet were within the city either south or west or neighbouring. So Bahati was in good hands as far as her friends/work friends were concerned. She was very pretty and friendly also.

The job her father's friend got her at a university (*her first bridge to cross*). And even though she stopped her education at GCSE Level, Bahati

had to sharpen quick because all her new contacts were intellectuals at the university and the work
itself was intellectually challenging.

That did not stop the girls have fun every weekend. She remembers one time they went to a very nice restaurant, and she was so shocked because she had never been in a restaurant as beautiful as that particular one.

The food was beautifully made the environment

was classic. As Bahati got to know Nairobi she was really thriving I mean she was zoning out of her shell, looking so pretty and getting really popular. She gained many friends.

SUPPORTING HER FAMILY

All the time Bahati never stop thinking about her siblings back home in the rural area. Since the family was so poor back home, always thinking about them and worrying about them was having bad effect on her.

After She started the new job, she started helping the family by sending them the money. The salary she was getting was so little she cannot believe it now in this day and time.

Anyway, the money went a long way she thinks it was the rate of inflation at that time. To be honest

the amount Bahati was getting per month was equivalent to £300 of today's money.
It was enough for rent food transport and supporting the family back home. The support needed back home for Bahati family was school fees for the two siblings that she was supporting and some money for her father.

The most difficult period was for her paying the school fees for those two siblings in secondary school. This was from the first year of secondary school, form one to form four. Her partner was helping her as he was a very good man.

The other sibling was being educated by a charitable firm that used to take a couple of kids every year.
This charitable firm operated in a system that if they pay school fees for a kid, that kid works for them every school holiday. That means it was like a child labour and that the child never got enough time to play outside or socialise with the other kids during school holidays.

The only things her dad needed to buy was bar soap, cooking oil sometimes sugar (very optional) and fuel for lighting (again very optional). Literally the things that are not grown in the farm.

Everything else Bahati's family needed for feeding was from the farm. The clothes were really torn up and embarrassing.

The life was tough but everyone else seem to be living in the same area with and just getting on. During those days, everyone in their surrounding villages were living the same peasant life, with wooden houses and no healthcare or enough food or so to speak not balanced diet.
As a young child, Bahati was wondering how life can be so difficult, God has his own way of divine intervention. Again, she did not know better, and her imagination had not been stretched to full capacity to imagine what was better than what she already had, which was her dad brothers and sisters, the hut (house) and farm animals.

Those farm animals were catering for milk, meat and school fees money when sold.
Bahati's household was not in a good way. The peasant life was too much to bear but there was seemingly no way out.

No one knew what was in God's plan, for those children that were growing with no clothes and shoes and not enough food and without a mother. Bahati used to be given any dress size by friends and she would wear them regardless of size she was humble and gracious. The shoes she was being given by anybody who sympathised with her and would be any size from adult to child size, and she would take and wear them.

This taught Bahati how to be humble. What she wanted did not matter to anyone, she was only an abstract only, but God had other plans. After migrating to UK, she realised that developed countries have their own poverty e.g., food bank and living on benefit which in itself poverty.

After the opportunities that came the way of Behati's family, no one could believe what God had done and continues doing so. But the home was a happy one, peasant but happy. This is the reason every time Bahati travels to Nairobi from London, she will carry all unwanted clothes and shoes and she would give them to the first person looking needy, just as people used to give to her in her earlier life.

Oblivious it was a bliss for her to see someone smiling and appreciating nice gifts that they were needed. She and family were just happy until that big moment hit them.The light was starting to shine at the end of the tunnel. Big sister/daughter working in Nairobi, wow it was a big breakthrough for the family. So Bahati started being the main support of the family.

From food to school fees that was required, the dad was sending request to Bahati to send whatever money, however small, to support the family.

Bahati was sharing a room with 5 other girls because they were all cutting cost by sharing and supporting the family back at their villages. Within the group of 5 friends, Bahati was the only one from the neediest home, I mean poor. In the evenings all the girls who shared the room with Bahati would talk stories from their own villages and life experiences. The stories were so juicy regarding school friends, boyfriends and who was better in different academic subjects, and which school they all attended.

Some girls had not experienced the poverty like the others. For example, the girl who became Bahati's best friend was from a well-off family. Her name was Raha. She used to invite Bahati to her home somewhere near Nairobi at a place called Ngecha.

The family liked Bahati a great deal and keep asking her to visit her whenever Raha was going to see her parents. They had a sympathetic ear, Bahati's mum had died, they could not comprehend the idea that
 Bahati did not have a mum and her dads house weren't as good condition as theirs.
Bahati had no one to go to in the weekend when others visited the village.

BAHATI'S FRIEND RAHA

Anyway, now Raha started asking Bahati to take
her to the village where she came from, but
Bahati would not accept since bahati's house was
just a wooden house like a big shed.
The two girls had a world of difference since
Raha's parents had an actual stone house and
electricity, same as the city.
Whereas bahati's home was just a wooden with
holes and no electricity or water at that time. So,
the friendship was being undermined by the fact
that Bahati did not want to take her best friend
back to her village.

The condition of the "house" was very bad it could
have embarrassed Both girls. Raha would have
been shocked to see the condition her friend's
family was in.

In the meantime, both girls, Bahati and Raha met
boyfriend/suitors that they were romancing and

before long, they both got pregnant and married their respective boyfriends. Raha's boyfriend was a young man who was studying in UK before returning to Nairobi to settle down.

Bahati met a young man who was registering to study a master's degree to further his education. He was a lovely man. So Bahati moved in with her boyfriend at the same time as Raha who also met with her new boyfriend. From there the girls remained good friend as they lived a separate married life.

There were no weddings or anything. If either girl asked for a wedding before babies, the prospect of marriage might have disappeared because these boyfriends did not have money for the wedding at the time.

During that time of extreme poverty, if you seemed needy you were to be disposed of with an easier going girl. Both girls got their two first babies, Bahati got two girls and her friend Raha got two boys.

SHE HAD A BABY

Bahati had a baby girl after 9 months as usual and had good time with her best friend Raha's in Nairobi living with her mature student boyfriend/husband. The pregnancy was going very well with no problem as far as health was concerned. Bahati's man was very happy and treating her very well in all aspects.

The pregnancy came to the final stages and Bahati was taken to Kenyatta National Hospital, Nairobi where all her husband's friends were working as doctors. The reason was that his baby was going to be delivered by his friends as doctors who had chosen to study medicine while Mark, Bahati's husband, studied as a Systems Analyst and worked in a bank. Bahati was very well looked after in the maternity ward.

The baby was very beautiful and in good health thanks God. Her husband was very happy and from that moment on, he was very serious as a family man financially and emotionally and physical support. Happy family happy life.

BAHATI STAYED AT HOME 3 MONTHS FOR MATERNITY

Bahati stayed at home on maternity leave while Mark went to his job. He made sure there was support for Bahati by getting a house girl to help around in the house with cooking and cleaning.

Time went so quickly it was soon time for Bahati to go back to work after maternity leave which was only 3 months at the time. It was emotional to go back to work and leave the baby at home, and it was difficult not to return to work as well.

Bahati had an option of using the house girl to look after the baby.

Returning to work was helpful as well because she had time to discuss motherhood and married life with other women.

Having just had a baby and being 19 had its advantage and disadvantages. Advantage was that after the baby, Bahati was looking so beautiful her skin was so smooth and glowing, her hair was full like a crown and let's say, she was thriving just like her baby was.

Her husband was looking after her and her house girl was helping her in the house – win-win situation for Bahati.

A man known as Peter, her boss was starting to admire and give her unwanted attention and that's something she did not want to engage in. Bahati liked her job because it was extra help, so she had a serious word with another boss, and she was transferred to another department away from the boss who was giving her unhealthy attention.

Life was looking promising for Bahati flourishing into a family girl. Time was going fast and before she knew she was pregnant again with her second baby. She was still supporting the family back
home in the village by paying school fees for two siblings, it was difficult. Working life was good because she was able to be a wife, mother and provide support to the other family members.

Bahati and her best friend got pregnant at the same time again for the second baby. Raha for a second boy and while Bahati got a second girl. Bahati was working and hustling in Nairobi looking after the kids, with the help of house-help maid.

The enjoyed every spare time together talking about their babies, husbands and the extended family. When her last born baby was four years old her husband came home one evening and announced that the whole family will relocate to London.

Bahati was shocked so much because as much as the news were good, news, she had never been away from her family.
Furthermore, she was the bread winner because the family looked up to her for financial support.

BIG CHANGES OCCURRED FOR BAHATI

At this time Bahati had left the job at the university and started working at a large Bank in Nairobi. It was one of the biggest banks in Nairobi it's still operating at a very good profit.

Her husband said he'd found a way of going to live abroad in UkK. Bahati did not realise that these plans were going to change her and her family's
 life for good. UK had prospects to succeed and make more money.

Problems started when they started making those arrangements for her to travel abroad to the UK.

Bahati accepted all those new changes regarding relocation, but it was coming at a cost. It meant that she will not see her father and sisters and brothers for a very long time.

Bahati's husband instructed her not to tell anyone that she was going to travel. That was a big problem. She refused and said that she is going to tell all her friends and family.

Any way Bahati went ahead and told all her friends that she was going abroad. Her husband allowed her to travel to the village to tell her father and immediate members of her family that she was travelling. So again, the argument was over the roof.

So Bahati won the argument and told everyone she wanted to tell that she was "going on the plane" abroad. While Bahati was at the village to say 'goodbyes' to her village friends and family, she heard that there was a funeral for her primary school head teacher, and she decided

to attend. That was the best decision she made to attend the funeral. She cherished the decision   for
a very long time. There at the funeral, she met literally anyone she knew in her life.

She met people who have known her from when she was born, and they were very excited to see a now so beautiful young girl from Nairobi. (From the poor girl they knew before to the new polished girl).They did not even know that the green grass was going to be even greener for Bahati from now on. They were like 'if your mum was here today to
see you '... (remember her mother had died some years back).

The village people were laterally very shocked at how Bahati looked beautiful, healthy and well dressed and on top of that she was going further. Bahati was a very slender tall girl, like she needed a bit of meat on her bones. Inside bahati's heart she was just thanking God that she was at that point and place in her life. Bahati was staunch a Christian girl. If it wasn't her faith, she could not have survived the temptations she met on her journey to where she is now as it was a lot. Every time she had alone moment, she would pray and thank God for all what He had done for her.

For having got a chance to leave the poverty-stricken village and transited to the two big city, Nairobi and London, for finding a job, for finding a good husband and having two children was a big achievement. And now an even better chance to go to the UK. It was like there was a hidden angel guiding her through the dark tunnels of death and poverty to a bright light.

At that time Bahati did not know that the UK was the best country in the world that you can go to live and make it. She did not even realise the great chance she had gotten.

Her husband knew this too because he was well travelled and had completed his master's degree.

In any case this going abroad could have been anywhere in the world according to her.
Bahati had not known whether the country was developed or not developed at that time of her life, she was just too remote and surviving, lacked geography skills and was consumed in self grief and self-pity. It could have been India, China or Europe. Bahati did not know which country had great opportunities. She only realised when she got in London. All she knew was that she was in the wrong country for survival.
What else could a girl want?

GOING TO LONDON

The big day arrived and now it was that big moment for Bahati to travel to London. So, the deal was that she leaves all her life behind and travel to London. To do this she had to take her smallest child with her. At the time the smallest child was three years old just approaching age four. The bigger child was six and approaching seven. So Bahati left one child and She was allowed in the UK. She had spending money in cash, she had a letter of invitation and was l ooking for the exact version of a tourist.

She was carrying a Harrods bag and she did not know it was the most distinguished and expensive store in London and her child was well dressed.
Her husband had brought her the Harrods bag and told her to carry it.

After 4 weeks, her husband put the six-year-old daughter on the flight to London, to go and meet her mother at Heathrow airport as Bahati and her husband had agreed. It was not difficult for a child to travel alone. He just pays extra fee for the lone child and the air hostess take care of the child and they check the child out and make announcement for the parent to meet at certain airport gate.

Bahati was at the gate waiting for her other daughter to arrive escorted by air hostess. It was a very happy moment when she met her daughter.

As good sounding as coming to London was, Bahati was not going to stay in London if her other daughter did not join her in London.

Bahati is a very maternal woman, and she could not have survived without her children.

From when she was young, she can remember praying to God that when she is old enough, she could have children. Thanks goodness this came to pass by God's Grace.

Her husband had travelled to London for business many times before (that's where the travelling idea was born from) and brought Bahati the Harrods bag and some clothes for her and the kids.

But to be honest she did not know what Harrods was whether it was a market or shop. So, the Harrods bag really made the Customs Officer think that Bahati was a girl of substance, and she was allowed to enter the United Kingdom.

All the requirements were met at Heathrow airport, she had a couple of hundreds of pounds spending money. She had no idea that that money was a lot those days.
But all said and done, the country was not economically or politically stable and Bahati was making the correct choice

The first week after she arrived. Bahati was filled with excitement, happiness and anxiety. The husband of the lady who had invited her came to meet her at the airport. It was her most exhilarating short journey in her whole life. It was like a movie
to her. The buildings and the smooth roads with more lanes than she had seen before in her life.

She just could not look away from the window.
She could have kissed the ground but

was too embarrassed. When Bahati reached to
the house of the family that had invited her,
it was not exciting any more. The sleeping
arrangements were not as expected.
They had a two-bedroom house and two boys
who were a bigger and loud than Bahati's girl and
there was not enough space for her and the little
girl. The house was small and Bahati was
surprised and shocked because the house was
two bedrooms
and crowded. Bahati just left Nairobi at
Westlands, Muthithi Avenue, a well affluent area
of the city. So she felt an immediate
downgrade.That was the first shock. Bahati's little
girl did not stop crying, she
was tired, sleepy and missing her sister and dad.
The host lady was not happy. Her name was
Teresa, she was irritable, and her husband kept
asking why Bahati's little baby kept crying. Their
two boys were big and independent. They had
forgotten how it is for a small toddler missing her

dad and sister and surrounded by strangers felt
like for her.

SETTLING IN LONDON

Bahati and her daughter Shiloh felt strange the
morning after. She was missing her dad and
sister Cicoh. Bahati did not know the process of
living in a foreign country, the process or
understood the requirements but she managed to
find out the process.
After 2 weeks her baby girl cicoh was put on the
plane and came safely to join her and Shiloh in
UK. The process was so long, Bahati wished if
she could just take a fight and go back home, but
she couldn't. By this time, it was too late because
Bahati had left her job back in Nairobi at the bank,
her husband had changed his mind about coming

to join her and it was just too much. (For him to change his mind taught her not to trust anyone

when planning her life) She got played by her husband, but it worked out for the best.
She decided to just be brave and stay. She made her mind up that she will leave that old life behind, she will succeed and prosper and that's exactly what happened. So Bahati got a school for the kids and got a job for herself. Those days it was so easy to get a job. She was even able to open a bank account with her with the papers allowing her to
stay in the country.
Everything was coming up as expected. She was so young but very bright. So, she was trying to mix with older people so that she could get useful information and advice.

By this time, Bahati had settled physically and mentally, and she looked beautiful and smart. Looking good was important to Bahati because she had looked rugged and unclean for a long time during her young period.

When she realised that working got her out of poverty, she never stopped working.

She had a quote by one of American president saying, "hard work never killed anybody" and she literally had that quote on the wall near the door.

Bahati had started working with an agency who booked her to work in two different shifts. Those two shits changed Bahati's life. Both of these shifts were a civil service posts on temporally terms. At one of these posts, she managed to be employed permanent, which changed her life and the other one she managed to get life partner who is still with her as she writes this book.

Life has surprises. They clicked and loved each other, and they moved in together. They are still together. She got a baby boy for him and named him Addis.

This person she met changed her life as he literally showed her with everything from driving around London, shopping and being a father

figure for her girls as they were very young and also bought her a new car to use as she liked. This whole luck changed Bahati's life completely. This partner has been Bahati's actual other half in the sense that he does not oppress or order her around, he is the most respectful person she has ever met.

He can, and likes cooking and when Bahati is unwell, he literally takes over cooking and everything else need doing after work.
He is not the type to be shouting around the house because he worked and prepared dinner

in the evening. Bahati had a sick hand, so her partner had been very understanding. This chapter is covered in *Bahati's Health*

Thinking of the Family left behind

Bahati started missing her family members immediately after arriving in UK but there was nothing she could do.
Bahati helped get her dad to clear his debts of his land that was stressing him. Her dad had a big farm, but he was not meeting his repayment and the bank was issuing notices of intent to repossess. This was the most stressing thing on Bahati's mind.

Immediately she started saving every penny she got and when the money was enough, she sent it through a trusted person.

That trusted person took Behati's dad the required money, they both went to Nakuru lands office and cleared the whole bill at once. Thanks God that matter was out of the way for her.

Some type of farm vegetables that Bahati loved eating when she was young.

Her dad relaxing and enjoying looking at his farm
products In

HUMBLE MAN AND BLESSED

Beautiful house that Bahati build for her dad

This was weighing heavy on Bahati's mind and immediately she got the money in UK Pounds that was the first thing she paid.
It was difficult to send money those days it was taking two weeks to send money bank to bank. Any way she managed to send money to her

dad, and he paid his debts which were distressing him a great deal. Bahati's dad was very happy and appreciated because he was owing people left and right, but the land was the most pressing issue because it nearly got repossessed.

Bahati missed her dad so much, every day she prayed for him to live long so that when she got her travel in order, she would have a chance to meet him again.
Her faith helped her to cross that line in her life. Those prayers were answered when she travelled back to her dad and he still alive and was waiting.

Bahati's new man knew London well in and out because he had lived there a few years before she arrived. She had arrived in London in early 90s in her 20s. She started new arrangement just to support friends and family, but Bahati was not a very good judge of character to surround herself with.
Bahati remembers when she brought her family member and instead of being cleared at airport, Bahati received a call that her family member was held at the airport, so she called a solicitor

and went straight to the airport. It took time for the solicitor to arrange and make their way to the airport it was in the afternoon. The airport staff

were so slow they did not call Bahati and the solicitor until Midnight. Bahati's family member was brought out by the airport officers and then released as soon as 20 minutes. It was so difficult when the officer was questioning this family member. Anyway, that's what the airport officers do that's their job.
If you contradict yourself at the airport, then you will be questioned and delayed. Anyway, the airport officers were tired, and they just let him in the
family member said he just want to visit London but couldn't say who invited him, he nearly got sent back. After that, she manages to bring many more families members to United Kingdom.

Bahati was very excited for her family member to have made it after 30 hours from start of the journey to finish. The first thing he wanted was to have a shower, a meal and a drink.

His shoes went straight in the bin as they had been worn enough for 30 to 50 hours being worn. He was bought a new pair of Clark shoes by Bahati's partner.

This was just a beginning and before long Bahati had brought many members of her family from the poverty and struggling life of the village. She had this dedication and blessing from higher powers to succeed single handily succeeded.

She was and is still a very family and friends-oriented woman and life had taught her that family matters most. She learned that loyalty lies within the family only after experiencing a short lively period in London. She has since realised that its easier said than done and some families members are grateful, and others are not.

What she did not realise is that loyalty and memory don't last long. Most people don't remember that
the bridges they burned will ever be needed again, the bridges were easily burned out and forgotten
by some of those families. Bahati's children were so young at the time when she was busy supporting her extended members
of her family and this was very difficult financially, but she was focused on helping.

She thought that giving is very important because, according to her experience, the more she gave the more she was being blessed and more doors were actually being opened for her and *that is a testimony for her*. Whatever Bahati set out to do, it would easily happen. Her faith and believes helped her a great deal.

Even though Bahati has been very successful in everything she had set out to do, she has learned through the had way that life can be difficult when she herself wanted emotional support down the line and those people were not available for emotional support that she might have needed.

This is because even after too much dedication to supporting family, it doesn't end so well because as you all know, you can choose friends, but you cannot choose family. Some of family she was dedicating herself so much dropped her like a hot metal once they settled well in London. She was shocked that they did not want to communicate with her anymore but then maybe they can reason out that Bahati helped them out of her will. There are lovely family members who appreciative, but some aren't as gracious as expected. The experience
was bittersweet.

The life was good. Bahati was working very hard, and her children were also and excelling in school in all subjects, she had her new partner and driving her own car.

Bahati had many friends, and they were all partying every weekend as you know that's what young people do.

The car Bahati was driving was old and breaking down all the time and was not safe. Repairing the old car was difficult for a woman because the mechanics charges too much money when it's a woman presenting herself in garage.

She realised that the economical way is to start trading in old cars for a newer car to keep up with

the trend and reduce mechanical expenses. she never stopped that trend. Now Bahati became a gadget girl and a taste for nice and expensive brand-new premium, and several other high-profile cars as she has worked hard, and God has blessed her in every way. The first time Bahati bought a car, she was having panic attacks by just looking at the car.

The reason was that the London roads are so confusing and so many roads that its easy to miss your turning. The other thing was that Bahati was waiting for her immigration paper to come through.

Driving is one thing of exposing yourself to the police if you haven't been allowed to remain. Most people were caught by police and returned to their motherland quickly. See immigration chapter below.
Prayers and believing in God been the driving force in everything she has done.
She cannot forget her humble beginning to where she is now despite trials and temptations. She has her moments when she worried about how she is

blessed and what is next in line of blessing and calamity especially physical health for her and her family and friends. Her children worked well in school and passed all their exams.

The two daughters and a son of Bahati, Shiloh and Cicoh and a boy called Addis, who also started driving age 17, graduated and started working.
She instilled in them that driving in a sign of freedom and safety as the city can be dangerous for teenagers and all the children were

driving and had cars by the age of 17. This is because she worried for the safety of her children when they were out but if driving, then she knew they will be safe.

These kids made Bahati a very proud mother with their obedience and choice of life they have made. This did not just happen, there was a lot of obstacles and hard work along the way. Bahati's children did not know the poverty she went through as a child, so she has tried her best to educate them.
Most teenagers and young adults especially boys fall in the Wrong groups and ends up dead.

This is a very big problem in UK most mothers are worried every day. This is another story for another book.
Ironically, Bahatis children are addicted to shoes. They be obsessed with shoes, and I mean they have so many pairs and its ironic they have never walk bare foot like their mother did when she was young in rural village of Kenya.

As mentioned in earlier chapters, Bahati got her first shoes when she was attending secondary school. So, every time she is travelling to Kenya, she carries suitcase full of shoes and another suitcase full of clothes to give to the needy kids in her rural village.

The kids or anyone who get this gift appreciates so much it reminds her of the day as she was young and on the receiving end of hand- me -downs. Another thing she notice with her kids is that there is a kind of telepathic thinking between her, and her children and it comes out in the way they like/and act like her when she was young. Bahati's children are generous, kind, loyal and bright.

CHILDREN'S EDUCATION AND SETTLING IN

Bahati's two girls settled well in primary school and were bright. The education system was very different from the one Bahati was educated in

Kenya, so she had to familiarise herself with the whole curriculum system.The British education system seems like one or two grades below what Bahati was familiar with. So, schooling her kids was much easier and more manageable.

The children settled well in school and coped well with their schoolwork. They were very confident and fitted in well. The teachers were always telling Bahati what a delight and pleasure it was to teach them as they were bright children. The children remained at the top sets of the class in studies, and homework was done without much trouble. Education was always at the centre of the household, and Bahati encouraged learning.

The house was full of encyclopaedias books and dictionaries. Bahati worked hard so that the family could have a computer at a time when computers in a private household were not common at all. She also ordered internet for the children to search topics for learning. The teachers were always impressed at how advanced the children's homework was.

The children were computer literate and were very good at games consoles.
The neighbourhood children could not believe that in Bahati's house there was a new game every now and then. She was happy that the children's school life did not cause her concern. The children had a good sense of confidence which came from a stable home.

They had a close relationship with their mother. The other kids in the neighbourhood liked playing with Bahati's children and other friends from the area.

All her children went to top Universities in London. The graduation pictures are displayed in the hallway of Bahati's house, and she is very proud mother. This makes her a very accomplished mum and thanks God for how thinks have worked out.

IMMIGRATION ISSUES

Bahati being as clever as she was, she handled her immigration issues with ease. She hired a lawyer early on in life when the kids were still in primary school. Due to delays, when the matter went to the immigration courts, the judge allowed Bahati and the kids leave to remain.

This was because by that time the ten years had passed just like that. By this time the kids were living like @coming to America', full of joy excitement normal life and mere happiness. Nonetheless, it took ten years for the immigration papers to come through. It was a very awaited period for Bahati and the kids. The freedom to travel was now open and the whole family have

travelled the world extensively. The children love to visit Kenya to see their grand dad who is still alive and now in very old age.

This topic is so juicy it will have to be followed up in the next a series which I hope will enjoy very much.

WORKING AND ENJOYING LIFE LONDON

Working has been a good thing for its like her therapeutic treatment. She enjoys her life being busy and being out there helping other.
Bahati joined civil servant from the beginning, and she had remained there for all this time. Civil servant is a good employer especially for foreigners. From this job, Bahati had grown herself from a humble beginning to a very mature and successful woman.

As at a mid-twenty's young woman with two young kids and in foreign country, it was lot of growing up to do to fit in all activities.

Lucky for Bahati, everything she was trying was working out. This she can only thank God and her faith. The nursery and school were just near her house. That meant she could have a few hours to herself to do the house and at least catch up with some new friends, Shopping and cooking when not working when not working.

This stage in life went down quickly and before Bahati knew the kids were able to play and ride outside, allowing her to recap the next thing for the day. Bahati started having new admirers, new friend at work and outside work. Bahati being a very pleasant girl, most friends were inviting her to go out parties.

She was wise and she did not go out with everyone who requested because she realised there is danger always roaming around.

At this stage she chooses one young man admirer as a partner, and he was not a bad choice. Eddie, she mentioned him earlier he was a good man and
a good father figure to the kids. They are still together now which is a blessing in itself.

Bahati enjoys swimming and health clubs to keep fit and keep fit. She also loved going out to dance and she did this a few times a month with now her chosen group of friends. They would go to clubs in East London she and her friends used to visit and

another one in south London that they regularly visited. Those early days the entry fee was fifteen to twenty pounds at the door, but that life is all in the past.

Now Bahati is a born-again Christian with more important matters and only visits houses of worship and churches.

There was good laughter dancing a lot and catching up with friends. In all this Bahati did not forget God. She prayed twice a day thanking God for that far He has brought her and went to church every Sunday. Her girls attended Sunday school and started serving at the table and supporting the priest. This grounded the girls in their religious study and knowledge and foundation. They also feared God.

HEALTH PROBLEMS

First and foremost, Bahati developed a swelling on her right arm between the wrist and the elbow. She was not concerned as she did not think

anything of it. She had it checked and was told to go home and wait for the biopsy repot.The test/biopsy was done in the same hospital that Bahati was an employee. After a week, the surgeon himself decided to walk in bahati's department and call her aside with her manager. (Confidentiality
was bleached).

The surgeon said that the swelling was a type of a cancer known as sarcoma and that it's very dangerous if it spread it could kill within few years if untreated. Luckily, it never spread further than the localised area at the hand.
I kept this illness so quiet I did not want to tell or discuss it with anyone except when discussing it with my doctors and surgeons.

Bahati was started in a cancer treatment which included just incision of the area removing the tumour. This continued for a few years until it reached another level where radio therapy was needed.

When the tumour continued to return around the same area in the arm, then a local chemotherapy was tried and applied just to the arm and not to the rest of the body. This was like a pilot scheme and Bahati regret allowing it to happen on her because it was very painful and not effective at all. The treatment lasted only one year and then
the tumour grew back again so it was a very bad experience for her and the family, while she remained in ICU for three days at private unit of the hospital, that's how dangerous that treatment was.

The doctor had explained to her that the

treatment might work or not work. There was nothing to lose so that's why she agreed. Bahati has diagrams/pictures that she cannot share, and she does not like looking at them because they are horrific. There was nothing to lose by accepting this treatment because things were looking bleak
for her.

After a high dose of chemo was applied through the vein by the neck, the whole hand turned black. If this had leaked to the main body, it could have been an instant death. That's why Bahati was in acute ward and monitored by CCTV and a nurse for 3 days and night. After she went home, she felt breathlessness and an ambulance was called. She was rushed to the nearest hospital in London king's college hospital and a scan revealed a blood clot. She was quickly treated with some anticoagulants and was advised to start walking around to do some small exercises. The cancer returned on the same area and that was the time Bahati knew that she has had to let go of the hand.

Bahati accepted to let go of the arm, just above elbow, because now the regrowth of the tumour was occurring more frequently. 2019 just before (covid 2020 year) She had an amputation (a word she hates to mention) and closed that chapter

and opened a new one. The cancer has not s pread anywhere else, so she is fine Healthwise thanks God.

DISABLED LIFE

This book has been written using one hand because Bahati felt compelled to tell her inspiring life story and health experience to encourage others. It is very difficult to enjoy life without a right arm especially if you were right-handed like she was.

All her friends rallied around her and supported her immensely. They prayed together and encouraged her not to feel sorry for herself as it could be worse, the friends offered their moral support and encouraged her to be strong with normal life and
not to hide and succumb to depression. Bahati's faith and prayers has also helped to grow spiritually.

This was a very painful and depressing time for her and her family but together, they have collectively overcome it and accepted the

situation as Bahati herself is very strong-minded person considering where she has come from. Her faith has carried her through.

Bahati has decided to insert this verse because she is a God-fearing person.

2 Corinthians 12:9

But he said to me, "My grace is sufficient for you, for my power is made perfect in weakness." Therefore, I will boast all the more gladly of my weaknesses, so that the power of Christ may rest upon me.

The whole family, my grown girls and their brother from Eddie, their stepdad and the grand children were very distraught.

But they have faith as well that keeps them strong. Bahati's partner is ever so supportive even after this period of health problems. Their relationship is stronger than ever. Most of all, her church friends were so supportive, they took it to themselves to make sure Behati was physically and spiritually supported.
Bahati decided to be strong and get on with life.

At some time back before her own sickness, she had been very empathic toward towards other people. Bahati paid a hospital bills for a family

friend who was held in hospital, unless she cleared her hospital bill. It was huge bill, but she managed
to pay it for her, and the lady was discharged from hospital.

Back in Nairobi they don't discharge a patient unless they clear the hospital bill. The lady later died anyway but she was very grateful. One of Bahati's sister was taking care of the lady and

she was so appreciative of the help and blessed Bahati and her family for their kind gesture. This sick lady had so many children and a husband, she could not understand how the whole family could not help or support her.

Covid19 2020

Bahati returned to work in civil service job in January 2020 not knowing what was around the corner. Pandemic Covid19 hit the world, and nobody expected what was about to happen. World was shut down. People were told to stay at home, clean their hand and sanitise and use masks. Everyone watched it start in China, then Italy not realising that it would be covering the whole world.

This was unbelievable to everyone especially Bahati, who had stayed at home for 8 months recuperating from the *amputation* and she was

ready to tackle the world head on as an amputee at work only to go back home again.

Bahati has decided not to put any image of her sick arm before amputation because they are stressful images. From end of March 2021 Bahati returned home from work due to Covid19 and Lockdown. Everything was shut down again.

After 7 months everything went back to normal,

all shops and many flights opened up again in September 2020. Then January came in 2021 looking as gloomy lit and dull as can be.
But by 04.01.2021 the Prime Minister of England shut down all non-essential stores again as covid19 loomed everywhere in UK.

The moment everyone is at the point of completely stressful due to covid19 at the back

of everyone's mind. But when I don't want to come off the health issues what affected Bahati, she handled all the Covid19 crises very well. The family, thank goodness were safe, as many families had experienced grief.

CONCLUSION

Bahati had been through a lot of real-life trials and hardship in her life. Having been born into poverty and her alone and her believe in God manages to turn things round. Stage by stage of life, Bahati kept taking responsibility for her life and managed to make the correct decision of her life and succeeds in life.

Despite the amputation, of her right arm, Bahati's has managed to keep her job with the civil service.
Not only did she succeed but also support her family members who she had left behind in

poverty and brought them to UK. She managed to save every penny (instead of spoiling her two kids) to pay for flights for them to go and live with her in London. Bahati supported a lady friend who was unable to pay for her hospital bills.

The hospital was holding her title deed but after that help from Bahati, the woman was discharged, and her family given their tittle deed back.

She liked giving back to the community just as someone opened that first door that led to her success. She settled well in the most popular city in the world London and brought up her own 3 children very well. The children, Cicoh, Shiloh, and Addis have graduated and have jobs. Bahati and
her partner Eddie still together and supporting each other in every way. Bahati's life is truly inspiring the motivation of writing this book is to show how Bahati has managed to get herself from rags to riches (the point she is at the moment is her riches). Bahati's main achievement

was when she managed to construct a beautiful house for her dad (bless him). And she also managed to buy her own houses back home.

Every time Bahati goes back to her roots, she supported the people she knows who are still

living in the same situation. Throughout the period,
Bahati has paid countless school fees for different children family and friends and paid hospital bills for a family friend who was not able to leave hospital unless they cleared the bill. Bahati has always at hand to help out even though now she notices that some people want to abuse her generosity and good intention.

Bahati is very religious and believed in serving others. The fact that someone is poor when young does not mean that they cannot turn

things round. Hard working, self believe, motivation, faithfulness and humbleness is important. This book is written as an inspiration and encouragement for someone to have a positive attitude and push themselves out of their comfort zone and find a path that works for them.

Bahati has always wanted to write this book since she was a young girl because she felt compelled to tell her story and inspire someone.
The lifestyle in her early life was extreme compared to what she has come to experience later in life.
She had written the script and then changed her mind, and the script went in the bin during one of her spring clearing. Bahati did not let her previous lifestyle define her, but it motivated her to where she is now.

The lesson here is that even though some people do not appreciate or remember the support or

help, do not ever fail to help and inspire because of a previous bad experience. Bahati has interpreted her early years of pure poverty to discipline and hardworking and taught her 3 children the same discipline. Never give up on your dreams. Life is a journey everyone has to follow.

Please lookout for a second series 2

Printed in Great Britain
by Amazon

65471765R00052